MW00941710

HEBRAIC
ETHICS:
Concepts For Better Living

ZEBULON BEN LEWI
HEDEQYAH

Copyright © 2015 Bayt Agoodah Publications

All rights reserved.

ISBN-13:
978-1517166489

ISBN-10:
1517166489

DEDICATION

TO YAH...

CONTENTS

682. 867.
7394

ACKNOWLEDGMENTS

TO ALL OF YAH'S SERVANTS WHO SEEK OUT
THE PATHS OF THE ANCIENTS…

QAM YASHARALA/QOOM YISRAEL!!

INTRODUCTION:

"**HEBRAIC ETHICS: Concepts For Better Living**" is a work intended to assist the servants of YAH in their daily application and living of Towrah. The principles contained in this book are NOT meant to be authoritative (only TOWRAH is "authoritative"); instead, this book should be viewed as a manual of ethical maxims to bring Towrah principles into everyday practical usage. Many of our people are not Towrah scholars, Hebrew language experts or the like. Most of our people are simply hungry souls trying to learn Towrah; not to offer scholastic, philosophical treatise, but to simply LIVE it....to make it relevant in real time. To quote the honorable Ben Ammi Ben Israel:

> "The true worship of God is an entire way of life, a continuous action, from the meal you eat in the morning, to the job you work on. It encompasses your every deed and thought."

Philosophical musings and theological rhetoric means nothing if the average man or woman are unable to visualize how to **apply** Towrah. This is one of the main reasons our people are in SIN: they simply do not know how to practically keep Law, especially in the lands of the captivity! Therefore, we who are referred to as "Teachers of the people" must always keep in mind that teachings which are not readily understood are useless to the person you are teaching. The teachings may have value later on down the road, but it has no value to the student in the "here and now". Our People must be afforded every opportunity to not only HEAR the Towrah but to UNDERSTAND the Towrah:

> **NEHEMIAH 8:6-8** "And Ezra blessed YHWH, the great Elohiym. And all the people answered, Amen, Amen, with lifting up their hands: and they bowed their heads, and worshipped YHWH with their faces to the ground.
>
> Also Jeshua, and Bani, and Sherebiah, Jamin, Akkub, Shabbethai, Hodijah, Maaseiah, Kelita, Azariah, Jozabad, Hanan, Pe laiah, and the Levites, **caused the people to understand the law:** and the people stood in their place.
>
> **So they read in the book in the law of Elohiym distinctly, and gave the sense, and caused them to understand the reading.**"

In writing this book, let it be understood that by no means is this work something I "conjured up" out of my mind and am now presenting it as some sort of "revelation". Quite the contrary, this book is a collection of tried and true concepts that I developed over the past 25 years. More importantly, it is the end result of sitting at the feet of my many Teachers, listening intently to their wise words, their in-depth breakdowns and the personal examples they led by. I am a product of many Camps and schools of thought because my Teachers were products of many Camps and schools of thought.

Therefore, I give honor and praises in the name of the Most high YHWH to all the Elders in Yisrael, from the ancient past to our current times. Everything I am is what you already were. I am grateful and I am thankful.

SHALOWM

THASHIYA MUSAR MANHAYGUWTH

(THE 9 PRINCIPLES OF LEADERSHIP)

1. You must always be ahead by way of knowledge of all those you lead.

Proverbs 24:5 "A wise man is strong; yea, a man of knowledge increaseth strength."

Ecclesiastes 1:16 "I communed with mine own heart, saying, Lo, I am come to great estate, and have gotten more wisdom than all they that have been before me in Jerusalem: yea, my heart had great experience of wisdom and knowledge."

2. You must be ever vigilant in keeping ahead of those you lead, by gathering the latest and the most accurate information for which they are searching.

Proverbs 1:5-6 "A wise man will hear, and will increase learning; and a man of understanding shall attain unto wise counsels: to understand a proverb, and the interpretation; the words of the wise, and their dark sayings."

3. You must have personality. This means, in your everyday dealings, you should possess typical patterns of speech, attitudes, needs, characteristics and behavior in coincidence to others in their

cause or activities.

Ben Sirach 44:2-4 "YHWH hath wrought great glory by them through his great power from the beginning. Such as did bear rule in their kingdoms, men renowned for their power, giving counsel by their understanding, and declaring prophecies: Leaders of the people by their counsels, and by their knowledge of learning meet for the people, wise and eloquent are their instructions:"

4. **You must NEVER teach lies to those you lead. False doctrine always reveals itself and your leadership will come to an abrupt end.**

Proverbs 29:12 "If a ruler hearken to lies, all his servants are wicked."

Proverbs 13:5 "The righteous hate what is false, but the wicked bring shame and disgrace."

5. You must, under all circumstances, carry yourself as an "Ark of Wisdom", but refrain vehemently from arrogance.

Proverbs 8:13 "The fear of YHWH is to hate evil: pride, and arrogancy, and the evil way, and the froward mouth, do I hate."

1st Samuel 2:3 "Talk no more so exceeding proudly; let not arrogancy come out of your mouth: for YHWH is a Elohiym of knowledge, and by him actions are weighed."

6. You must not, and cannot afford to, mix yourself up with anything or anyone that has no intention of becoming dignified, self -respecting and morally grounded in the Instructions of YAH.

Ben Sirach 37:12 "But be continually

with a righteous man, whom thou knowest to keep the commandments of YHWH, whose, mind is according to thy mind, and will sorrow with thee, if thou shalt miscarry."

7. **You must be self possessed, confident and self reliant. When those following you see this, they will trust in and follow your example more easily.**

Joshua 1:5-7 "There shall not any man be able to stand before thee all the days of thy life: as I was with Moses, so I will be with thee: I will not fail thee, nor forsake thee. Be strong and of a good courage: for unto this people shalt thou divide for an inheritance the land, which I sware unto their fathers to give them. Only be thou strong and very courageous, that thou mayest observe to do according to all the law, which Moses my servant commanded thee: turn not from it to the right hand or to the left, that thou mayest prosper whithersoever thou goest."

8. **You must always think before you speak or act, because what you do or say directly affects you and those you teach.**

Proverbs 17:28 "Even a fool, when he holdeth his peace, is counted wise: and he that shutteth his lips is esteemed a man of understanding."

Proverbs 18:13 "He that answereth a matter before he heareth it, it is folly and shame unto him."

9. **You must NEVER speak on anything you do not know about. You should always make sure that the proper research is done before speaking on any subject.**

Proverbs 15:28 "The heart of the righteous studieth to answer: but the mouth of the wicked poureth out evil things."

Proverbs 16:23 "The heart of the wise teacheth his mouth, and addeth learning to his lips."

Ben Sirach 11:7-8 "Blame not before thou hast examined the truth: understand first, and then rebuke. Answer not before thou hast heard the cause: neither interrupt men in the midst of their talk."

YAKHAD (UNITY):

As we travel through life, we are always being afforded the opportunity to make choices as it pertains to the directions we are inclined to go. There is the innate power of Free Will that the MOST HIGH has blessed us with. As life is full of pitfalls and windfalls, it is essential to make intelligent choices and decisions.

As individual Hebrews, we are able to acquire an abundance of power, knowledge, material possessions, etc.; but one person can never think they can acquire the same levels and quantities of these things that a UNIFIED COLLECTIVE can accomplish. A finger cannot boast against a fist; one finger will never have the same impact that a unified group of fingers will have.

2nd Chronicles 30:12 "Also in Judah the hand of Elohiym was to give them one heart to do the commandment of the king and of the princes, by the word of YHWH."

So to come together in unification makes us exponentially more powerful than if each one of us moves alone. Even if the Hebrew Nations' "unity" isn't as strong as it should be internally, we should NEVER allow it to appear that way on the outside! When we consider how much damage the Enemy has done to us in this captivity, the sheer fact that we are able to stand together in ANY manner is sufficient to cause the Enemy to reconsider how they will approach us and ponder whether THEY are strong enough to go against us.

However, we must ask ourselves a question: ARE WE IN FACT AS STRONG AS WE APPEAR TO BE? Is that strong unification present in our communities, our Congregation/Camps or even within ourselves? If your honest answer is "NO", then WHY NOT? If your honest answer is "YES", then PROVE IT.

Psalm 133:1 "Behold, how good and how pleasant it is for brethren to dwell together in unity!"

What are we doing individually to build and strengthen our Hebrew communities, Congregations, and our interpersonal interactions? Are our thoughts, words and actions reflective of this "strong unity" that we vociferously profess? Hebrews often speak against camps, claiming that the camp has done nothing for them. What they do not consider is that a camp can do no more for you than you are willing to put into that camp. A camp is not welfare, where you come in with a "Daffy Duck" attitude of "Gimme, gimme, gimmie" and "Mine, mine, mine". The question that should constantly be in the forefront of our minds is, **"What have I done personally to facilitate the great work of YAH in my camp, congregation, community and Nation as a whole**? Another question to ask ourselves is **"Are my efforts in this work going to**

fortify and strengthen me as an individual, so that I may in turn continue to fortify others with that same energy?"

This is one of the manners in which you empower your Nation. A Nation is only as strong as the collective members. The stronger the individual Hebrew becomes, the more invincible the Nation as a whole is to become.

There are those who may claim that "doctrinal issues" plays a major role in the lack of unification among Yisrael. While this is true in many respects, it is only a "top layer" issue and has no intrinsic form when one seeks "common denominator" matters to focus on. Consider Marcus Garvey and his UNIA organization; it was composed of members from a plethora of national and "spiritual" backgrounds. Everybody from Towrah Keepers, Moors, Muslims even down to various sects of Christians were members in the UNIA. Yet, the UNIA was able to thrive in the early 20th century because the focus remained on "common denominator" issues, such as economic development, building our own educational infrastructures, etc. Issues such as these did not require "across the board" agreement on doctrines; once the "common denominator" issues are settled and built up, all other "doctrinal discrepancies" could then be dealt with. Yisrael would do well to approach our "issues" in like manner. UNITY must be the focal point and result of all of our endeavors in the Truth.

AHABAH (LOVE):

Ahabah (Love) is a part of us, and it inevitably becomes a part of everything we do. In our everyday words and deeds, we reflect that which is contained within. We do this on a daily basis, usually without conscious thought. It is automatically initiated by a combination of our internal principles and our external environment.

There are many terms regularly associated with Love; there is attraction, admiration, desire, lust and infatuation. Are these terms the same as Love? Absolutely not. Nevertheless, how often do we use these terms interchangeably with Love? This is clearly based upon faulty and misguided definitions of love; we have long been taught that "love is a feeling" or "love knows no color" as if Love is an abstract concept of which one has no control of. When we believe these romanticized definitions of love, it becomes easy to understand how people can confuse love with the various terms listed above.

It has been said that "love is a decision"; while this may be true in many respects, the crucible of love goes beyond simply "deciding" to love and be loved. Indeed, a clear, tangible understanding of Love can be achieved by examining our relationship with the Most High. When we consider the Covenant between YAH and his people, it is a covenant based on a "give and take" platform. It is a covenant which suggests that true love is to be reciprocated and further illustrated through how we interact with Him and vice versa. Likewise, our love towards and for our wives, children, friends, family and Nation cannot simply be a "stand alone" decision. There must always be a further expression of this love through tangible, reciprocated acts and deeds. Deuteronomy 7:9 informs us:

"Know therefore that YHWH thy Elohiym, he is Elohiym, the faithful Elohiym, which keepeth covenant and mercy with them that love him and keep his commandments to a thousand generations;"

While it is possible to love without having it returned, reciprocated love is the highest and truest expression of it; as one empties themselves into the other, that same other refills them with that corresponding energy and the process continues. This is a prime example and reason why a person cannot truly love "material items" such as cars, homes, etc: cars and homes have no "soul", no life force in which to compliment the owner. These "things" are incapable of reciprocating the "love" and thus, the person will always find themselves "unfulfilled", even with an abundance of these luxuries.

Ahabah/Love is a powerful force (energy/spirit) and this "power" is often overlooked. It is through love that two parents decide to bring forth life, in spite of the probable hardships that arises because of it. It is love that drives a person to willingly jeopardize their lives for the lives of their spouse, children and other loved ones. It is this understanding of Love that must be at the forefront of our definitions and interpretations of the term; it must be manifested in persons' deeds as well as in their speech.

HATA'AMAH (CONFORMITY):

When we conform to anything, we cause it to become habitual. It becomes a part of our daily existence, being unable to distinguish it from the other elements of one's life. However, is there anything wrong with conformity? Is it necessarily a bad thing? On one hand, it's good and on the other hand, it not. This is obviously determined by what it is that we are conforming.

If we find ourselves partaking in negative and unrighteous activities on a regular basis, this will become habitual and thus conformity sets in. As an example, there are many people who indulge in profane speech, cigarettes/drugs, alcohol, fornication and a plethora of other vices that they KNOW are detrimental to themselves, yet they continue to practice these things. As the old saying goes, "Practice Makes Perfect".

On the other side of the spectrum, if we are partaking in more positive, righteous activities regularly, we can surely expect to reap the fruits of our labor, thus allowing for productive conformity. Activities such as healthy eating, holistic thinking, studying and applying Towrah, etc., all require a discipline that can only be achieved by rigid repetition. Again, "Practice Makes Perfect".

I have always been fascinated at how relatively easy it is for us to pick up negative habits, yet we seem to complain how difficult it is to develop positive ones. Some people have taken the position that "a person only does what their heart drives them to do". Perhaps on a rudimentary level, this may have some validity. However, since we are not monolithic in our thinking, we must consider that people tend to be influenced and molded by the dominant activities in which they find themselves exposed to.

Anyone who is exposed to a certain way of conduct for extended periods of time develops a greater chance of embracing that conduct; it's basic psychology. Therefore, <u>environment</u> (while not applicable in all situations with all people) plays a major role in the habits and conduct of a person. Nevertheless, the more disciplined and conformed we become in righteousness, the more powerful your resistance to negativity and wickedness becomes. Developing good habits and establishing strong mental and spiritual discipline is critical to living in this current life and helps us make better decisions going forward.

Embracing the idea of conformity as it pertains to life and better discipline is one thing, but it's not the "all end" of the matter. What's equally important (if not moreso) is the embracing of "the journey" and the manner in which you travel. We often forget that the INTEGRITY of how a person goes about living their lives supersedes the tangible accomplishments on that journey. It is not simply about "WHAT you do" but

HOW you do it and whether or not it was done with integrity.

Do not take your discipline (or lack of discipline thereof) for granted. They are the first thing perceptive people see when they get to know you. Words are important but discipline is crucial, especially when you are in a position of leadership or influence. **Hata'amah** (conformity) is necessary to establish this.

MAKH'SHABUTE (THOUGHTS):

As Hebrews, we are all too familiar with Proverbs 23:7a which states: "For as he thinketh in his heart, so is he:" It is a well known maxim, universally acknowledged as truth in most cultures outside of ours. However, like all lofty and high spiritual anecdotes, it may sound good but do we REALLY believe it? There are those of us who do understand and implement this concept into our everyday regimen. Nevertheless, there are those who have simply been unable (or unwilling) to grasp this concept as it pertains to their lives.

What determines the course of our lives? Some will say **external factors and circumstances**, while others will postulate that it is the **power of our thoughts** that control our lives. However, these two positions are not necessarily in opposition to each other, and it becomes evident when we consult the Scriptures. For instance, Qoheleth (Ecclesiastes) 9:11 tells us:

"I considered and observed on earth the following: The race doesn't go to the swift, nor the battle to the strong, nor food to the wise, nor wealth to the smart, nor recognition to the skilled. Instead, timing and circumstances meet them all."

Solomon teaches us in this passage that often in life, circumstances that are beyond our direct control may determine any given outcome. How many times have we observed a sporting event such as boxing, where the Champion (the clearly better fighter) loses the championship to a second rate, unknown fighter? I personally am reminded of the Mike Tyson-Buster Douglass match of 1990, where there is no logical explanation as to why Douglass beat Tyson. In boxing circles, it is considered a mystery, since Tyson (overall) was by far the greater fighter. However, as the above Scripture illustrates, it wasn't the "strong" that won the battle there; Douglass was in the right time and circumstance and took advantage of the opportunity. This is the nature of life.

On the other hand, we do in fact have direct control over other elements of our lives and the paths we may take. The Most High YAH informs us of the following in Deuteronomy 8:18:

"But you shall remember YAHAWAH your Elohiym: for it is he that <u>gives you power to get wealth</u>, that he may establish his covenant which he swore unto your fathers, as it is this day."

In this text, YAH exhorts us to keep Him in our thoughts at all times and that He implanted "power" in us to obtain wealth. This is of great importance because it illustrates the other extreme of what we observed earlier. If we have the power to get wealth (among other things), the implication is that we, in fact, can directly steer the course of our external undertakings in life. Let's consider another scripture, this time from Deuteronomy 30:19-

"I call heaven and earth as witness this day against you, that I have set before you <u>life and death, blessing and cursing: therefore choose life, that both you and your descendants may live:"</u>

Again, we are reminded by YAH (through Moses) that life in general is composed of choices.....choices in which can and does affect our "comings and goings". But even more important, is this teaching that each choice (good or evil) will yield its own specific blessing/curse, and we ourselves do have the power to control these choices and attract the best (or worst) possible outcomes.

Therefore, when we look at the initial concepts spoken of above, we come to the understanding that they are not two contradictory positions, but actually two branches of the same tree. The positions that "external factors and circumstances control our destiny" verses "the power of our own thoughts control our destiny" can never be separated from the one unifying factor….our MAK'SHABUTE (thoughts) mold our outer world as well as our inner world.

How we manufacture and utilize our thoughts have a direct and critical bearing upon our lives and the lives of others. Thoughts are energy and energy has the power to create or destroy. Therefore, we must develop discipline as it pertains to our thoughts and how we bring them into the world. Positive thoughts give life to positive outcomes and negative thoughts give life to negative outcomes. It behooves us to control our Mak'shabute/thoughts in a manner which is conducive to righteous living.

SHIYSHAH HIYBATIYM (6 FACETS)

1. Control Of Thought: Understand the necessity of thought regulation. Cultivate the habit of establishing order and correct sequence of your thoughts. In the scope of leadership, this becomes critical if one desires to lead souls to YAH. At all times, your thoughts must follow logical patterns of expression, so that your audience can follow a clear train of ideas and understand your platform.

2. Control Of Actions: Like the above quality, an equal amount of supervision must be employed as it pertains to our actions. Our actions and deeds are a natural extension of our thoughts; therefore, these actions should not only agree with our thoughts, but should follow the same logical order of expression.

3. Impartiality: The need to have trust and faith upon every Hebrew you encounter, until given a cogent reason not to. Often times we embrace the Eurocentric concept of "Trust no one, until they give you a reason to trust them", along with the old adage "Beware of Greeks bearing gifts". Subsequently, we are led to the tendency of taking a few "bad experiences" with fellow Hebrews and lumping them with innocent Hebrews we may come to know going forward. Therefore, ALL Hebrews pay for the actions of a few. These are examples of how Hebrews in the Diaspora have come to have a natural distrust for each other, via European influence. While this is not to suggest that every Hebrew CAN be trusted, it DOES suggest that every Hebrew must be afforded the benefit of the doubt. We must begin and continue to cultivate the spirit TRUST among our Nation.

4. Perseverance: The requirement of cultivating ones' endurance. In this anti-YAH world that we live in, it becomes very easy to fall into the habit of "giving up" when circumstances become difficult. Life can be full of these "pitfalls" and what appears to be "insurmountable odds" at times. However, if we are to accrue any amount of success in our undertakings (both personal and collectively as a Nation), we must be willing to fight for that success. When we are focused on the end results of our labor, the task itself must not be a hindrance. Struggle is only the "refining fire" on the way to Success. As a people who are residing in a worldwide captivity and trying to petition YAH to be returned to their Heritage, **perseverance** must be cultivated in the very souls of our people.

5. Equilibrium: The need to maintain your composure when being faced with any and all circumstances in life. We must discard the habit of fluctuating between great heights of joy and the lowest levels of sorrow. Of course, this is not saying that we should be emotionless beings, for this goes against the very nature of how were created. However, we should be learning how to control our emotions and use them for the appropriate reasons and times. It is a tragedy when we make crucial decisions premised on our "feelings" or when we're caught up in our emotions. When doing this, we suffer long term effects all because of short term feelings. We as Yisrael must reject this tendency to lean upon emotions and instead, approach all situations from a logical, well thought out perspective.

6. Forbearance: Having tolerance towards your Brothers and Sisters who may not be operating on the same wavelength as yourself. It is very easy to forget that the way we may have come into the Truth on any subject is not necessarily the same way another Hebrew came upon this Truth. We all process information at differing speeds and differing methods. We must continually keep in mind our own struggles coming into our awakening to YAH, and use that experience to offer empathy towards Brothers and Sisters who are currently struggling with their own trials. Just because many of us are no longer living a life of wickedness , it doesn't mean we are far removed from those days and we therefore must practice **forbearance** towards those who are younger in spirit.

KALALIY
HATH'NAHAGOYTH
(MAXIMS OF CONDUCT):

1. Refrain from the tendency to make assumptions about individuals and/or their circumstances.

Proverbs 18:13 "Whoever answers before listening is both foolish and shameful."

Proverbs 25:8 "Do not go hastily to court; For what will you do in the end, When your neighbor has put you to shame?"

2. Get into the habit of controlling your

anger/being upset and not giving others the "key" to those doors.

> *Ecclesiastes 7:9* "Be not quick in your spirit to become angry, for anger lodges in the bosom of fools."

> *Sirach 1:22-23* "Unjust anger won't be justified, for the tipping point of one's anger is one's downfall. Patient people will hold themselves back until the right moment, and afterward they will be paid back with joy."

3. Be cognizant of your surroundings and let nothing surprise you.

> *Proverbs 22:3* "The prudent sees danger and hides himself, but the simple go on and suffer for it."

4. Never finalize anything in life, for "Life" moves in cyclic patterns and evolves. What you don't see today may reveal itself in due season.

5. Always be considerate and mindful of people and circumstances.

> *Zechariah 7:9* "Thus has YAH of hosts said, 'Dispense true justice and practice kindness and compassion each to his brother;

> *Zechariah 7:10* "Do not oppress the widow, the fatherless, the sojourner, or the poor, and let none of you devise evil against another in your heart."

6. Never attempt to teach a lesson which you have not learned or mastered.

> *Sirach 37:19* "There is one that is wise and teacheth many, and yet is unprofitable to himself."

7. Practice what you preach; your words must embody corresponding actions.

> *Psalm 50:16-17* "But to the wicked Elohiym says: "What right have you to declare My

statutes, Or take My covenant in your
mouth, Seeing you hate instruction And cast
My words behind you?"

Isaiah 29:13 "Therefore YHWH said:
"Inasmuch as these people draw near with
their mouths And honor Me with their lips,
But have removed their hearts far from Me,
And their fear toward Me is taught by
the commandment of men,"

8. Focus strongly on the advancement of your physical, mental and spiritual health.

Proverbs 3:7-8 "Do not be wise in your own
eyes; Fear YHWH and depart from evil. It
will be health to your flesh, And strength to
your bones."

Proverbs 3:1-2 "My son, do not forget my
teaching, but let your heart keep my
commandments, for length of days and years
of life and peace they will add to you."

Isaiah 55:2 "Why do you spend your money
for that which is not bread, and your labor for

*that which does not satisfy? Listen diligently
to me, and eat what is good, and delight
yourselves in rich food."*

9. Be and remain consistent in all of your actions and how they influence other's perception of you.

*Ben Sirach 44:2-4 "YHWH hath wrought
great glory by them through his great power
from the beginning. Such as did bear rule in
their kingdoms, men renowned for their
power, giving counsel by their
understanding, and declaring prophecies:
Leaders of the people by their counsels, and
by their knowledge of learning meet for the
people, wise and eloquent are their
instructions:"*

10. Understand that your thoughts and words are equally as important and powerful as your actions.

*Psalm 141:3 "Set a guard, O YHWH, over my
mouth; keep watch over the door of my lips!"*

Ben Sirach 23:7 "*7 Hear, O ye children, the discipline of the mouth: he that keepeth it shall never be taken in his lips.*"

Ben Sirach 20:13 "*A wise man by his words maketh him beloved: but the graces of fools shall be poured out.*"

11. Be mindful that you are a link in the larger chain that makes up Yisrael. Your subsequent thoughts, words and deeds reflect just as much on your Nation as it does on yourself. We all play integral role in the upliftment and establishing of our Nation.

Ben Sirach 38:29-34 "*So doth the potter sitting at his work, and turning the wheel about with his feet, who is alway carefully set at his work, and maketh all his work by number; He fashioneth the clay with his arm, and boweth down his strength before his feet; he applieth himself to lead it over; and he is diligent to make clean the furnace: All these trust to their hands: and every one is wise in his work. Without these cannot a city be inhabited: and they shall not dwell where they will, nor go up and down: They shall not be sought for in publick counsel, nor sit high in the congregation: they shall not sit on the judges' seat, nor understand the sentence of judgment: they cannot declare justice and judgment; and they shall not be found where parables are spoken. But they will maintain the state of the world, and [all] their desire is in the work of their craft."*

12. You must acquire the conviction that the real " being of a man" doesn't simply exist in your exterior, but moreso in your interior.

1 Samuel 16:6-7 "When they entered, he looked at Eliab and thought, "Surely YHWH's anointed is before Him." But YHWH said to Samuel, "Do not look at his appearance or at the height of his stature, because I have rejected him; for Elohiym sees not as man sees, for man looks at the outward appearance, but YHWH looks at the heart."

Proverbs 16:12 *"All the ways of a man are clean in his own sight, But YHWH weighs the motives.*

13. You must be steadfast in identifying your goals and continuing to pursue them.

2 Chronicles 15:7 *"Be ye strong therefore, and let not your hands be weak: for your work shall be rewarded."*

Proverbs 16:3 *"Commit thy works unto YHWH, and thy thoughts shall be established."*

14. Always maintain a feeling of thankfulness for all that we are favored with by YAH.

Isaiah 12:4-5 *"And you will say in that day: "Give thanks to YHWH, call upon his name, make known his deeds among the peoples,* *proclaim that his name is exalted. "Sing praises to YHWH, for he has done gloriously; let this be made known in all the earth."*

Isaiah 100:1-5 *"Make a joyful noise to YHWH, all the earth! Serve YHWH with gladness! Come into his presence with singing! Know that YHWH, he is Elohiym! It is he who made us, and we are his; we are his people, and the sheep of his pasture. Enter his gates with thanksgiving, and his courts with praise! Give thanks to him; bless his name! For YHWH is good; his steadfast love endures forever, and his faithfulness to all generations."*

15. Your ideas and concepts must be guarded; each idea should possess significance for you. You should see in it a definite message instructing you concerning the things of the world around you.

Proverbs 4:23 "Keep your heart with all vigilance, for from it flow the springs of life."

16. Thoughtless and meaningless actions should be foreign to your platform. You should establish well considered grounds for everything you do and abstain from everything for which no significant motive is forthcoming.

> *Proverbs 15:28* "The heart of the righteous ponders how to answer, but the mouth of the wicked pours out evil things."

> *Proverbs 18:21* "Death and life are in the power of the tongue, and those who love it will eat its fruits."

17. Utter no word that is devoid of meaning. Be ready to converse with all Hebrews (conscious or unconscious), but do so thoughtfully and with thorough deliberation. Never speak without grounds for what you have to say. You should seek to use neither too many or too few words.

Ben Sirach 20:5-8 "There is one that keepeth silence, and is found wise: and another by much babbling becometh hateful. Some man holdeth his tongue, because he hath not to answer: and some keepeth silence, knowing his time. A wise man will hold his tongue till he see opportunity: but a babbler and a fool will regard no time. He that useth many words shall be abhorred; and he that taketh to himself authority therein shall be hated."

18. Regulate your outward actions. Adjust your actions so that they harmonize with the Truth you claim to represent. When an external motive causes you to act, consider how you can best respond. When the impulse proceeds from yourself, weigh with minute care the effects of your actions.

Ben Sirach 32:18-19 "A man of counsel will be considerate; but a strange and proud man is not daunted with fear, even when of himself he hath done without counsel. Do nothing without advice; and when thou hast once done, repent not."

19. In the management of your life, endeavor to live in conformity with YAH and his Towrah. Look upon life as an opportunity to serve YAH and your People and apply it accordingly.

1 Samuel 12:24 "Only fear YHWH and serve him faithfully with all your heart. For consider what great things he has done for you."

20. Seek to omit nothing that is within your grasp. See yourself as a vital wheel in the vast machine that is Yisrael. Seek to comprehend your specific purposes in life and to see life beyond the limits of triviality.

Psalm 8:4-6 "What is man, that thou art mindful of him? and the son of man, that thou visitest him? For thou hast made him a little lower than the angels, and hast crowned him with glory and honour. Thou madest him to have *dominion over the works of thy hands; thou hast put all things under his feet:"*

21. Learn as much from life as possible. Gather a rich store of experience and utilize it, along with Towrah, for counsel going forward. Therefore, do nothing without looking back upon experiences and Towrah from which you can derive help in your everyday decisions.

Ben Sirach 34:9-12 "A man that hath travelled knoweth many things; and he that hath much experience will declare wisdom. He that hath no experience knoweth little: but he that hath travelled is full of prudence. When I travelled, I saw many things; and I understand more than I can express. I was ofttimes in danger of death: yet I was delivered because of these things.

22. You must, from time to time, glance introspectively into yourself; sink back into yourself and take yourself carefully to task. You must form and test the

fundamental principles of life lessons; analyze in your mind the sum total of your knowledge and reflect upon the content & how it correlates with your direction in life.

Ben Sirach 18:20-21 "*Before judgment examine thyself, and in the day of visitation thou shalt find mercy. Humble thyself before thou be sick, and in the time of sins shew repentance.*"

ABOUT THE AUTHOR

Pedigree wise, Zebulon Ben Lewi Hedeqyah is of the BNAI ZAKEN Hebrew Yisraelite School "family tree", coming through the doors of "Camp Yakhad" (an offshoot of Bnai Zaqen) in the early 1990's, a camp led by the late Chief Amoz Ben Yehudah (may YAH be gracious towards his memory), (Chief) Prince Tsippor Ben Zevulun and Chief Of Chiefs Naphtali, among others.

One of the most important lessons Brother Zebulon learned in his early years at Yakhad was "the Love of Yisrael". To have undying love for your people is a requirement to serve YAH. Another important lesson learned was that "A doctrine can only be Truth if it can withstand scrutiny; otherwise, it is simply a belief."

Armed with these two principle templates (and many more), young Zebulon would continue to study diligently and seek out the Truth that was given to our Ancient Fathers:

"Thus says YAHAWAH, Stand in the Ways, and see, and ask for the eternal paths, where the good way is, and walk in it, and you shall find rest for your souls..." (Yirmeyahu 6:16)

In brother Zebulon's early journey, he began combing through the Scriptures, researching anthropological, historical and Theological works in addition to the Hebrew, Greek, Aramaic and Arabic languages, all the while asking The MOST HIGH (through prayer) to open his eyes of understanding. In the process of time, many young people would be attracted to the teachings of YAH through this brother and, subsequently, would desire to become students. Not taking this privilege lightly, Zebulon found himself overwhelmed by the responsibility of bringing the Truth of YAHAWAH to these young people, as he was himself young, both chronologically and spiritually. But understanding that YAH's people had to be taught, he was reminded of King Solomon's request to

YAHAWAH:

"And your servant is in the midst of your people which you have chosen, a great people, that cannot be numbered nor counted for multitude. Give to your servant therefore an understanding mind to judge your people, that I may distinguish between good and evil: for who is able to judge your great people?" (1st Kings 8-9)

It was in that spirit that Zebulon proceeded to work with others who were searching for themselves, not only showing them the Almighty YAHAWAH, but also the concept of loving their people........true brotherhood. After nearly 25 years, his understanding has evolved and is striving to go to the second level of being a Hebrew Yisraelite..........becoming a Servant of The Most High. All of his works and efforts in this life are to that end.

ZEBULON BEN LEWI HEDEQYAH

54388779R00034

Made in the USA
San Bernardino, CA
15 October 2017